Damaged Goods in

Black and White

Damaged Goods in

Black White *and*

AMERICA, *We Have a* PROBLEM

HAJJI WALI FURQAN

with appendix by Blase Boettcher

iUniverse

DAMAGED GOODS IN BLACK AND WHITE
AMERICA, WE HAVE A PROBLEM

iUniverse books may be ordered through booksellers or by contacting:

iUniverse
1663 Liberty Drive
Bloomington, IN 47403
www.iuniverse.com
1-800-Authors (1-800-288-4677)

ISBN: 978-1-4917-4769-8 (sc)
ISBN: 978-1-4917-4768-1 (e)

Library of Congress Control Number: 2014918522

Print information available on the last page.

iUniverse rev. date: 02/25/2016

Contents

Introduction

Faith, patience, and the doing of good deeds have been part of my family and community life for more than forty years. Getting to this point was a process, some of which is delineated in this book. Through that process, I have been able to define many shortcomings in our present culture, as well as steps that can be taken to improve these attitudes and deficiencies.

I am originally from a small town in northeast Arkansas. My mother chopped, picked, and pulled cotton in Arkansas during the summer and fall and would migrate to Florida during the winter months to support her family as a single parent. I graduated from an integrated high school in Arkansas and attended college in Kirksville, Missouri, at Northeast Missouri State University which is now known as Truman State.

I met my wife-to-be in college where we got married forty-one years ago. We are the proud parents of seven children, five girls and two boys. After graduation from college in 1974 with a BS degree in business administration, I moved to St. Louis, Missouri, where I would begin to work for corporate St. Louis. My wife joined me two years later with a master's degree in math. My wife and I are Muslims, converts to the religion Al-Islam, and five of our children attended the Clara Muhammad School at Al-Mu'Minun Islamic Center here in St. Louis. I made the pilgrimage to Mecca in 1980, an obligation on all able-bodied Muslims once in their lifetime, and I earned the right to add Hajji to my name.

My wife and I have been owners and operators of several restaurants in the St. Louis area. We have invested in and rehabbed several properties, including our present residence. I have been a mentor and a volunteer in the St. Louis Public School System. I have volunteered in the adult and juvenile correctional facilities in St. Louis and St. Louis County. I was both a volunteer and paid chaplain for the Illinois Correction Center in Menard, Illinois, for over twenty-five years. I am a certified hospice chaplain.

Four years ago I founded the organization known as PATOY. Parents can be and should be a tremendous influence in their children's lives. We believe "a parent's motivation is a child's inspiration." This is the motto of PATOY (Paying Attention to Our Youth), a 501-C-3 organization of which I am president and founder. Our organization places special emphasis on parental responsibility for the proper development of our children. If we, as a nation, are to become more aware of "damaged goods in black and white," then we must insist that our society, the parents of these youths, and the youths themselves should become more responsible for their actions.

Chapter 1

The Confrontation in Black, White, and Brown

I was a twenty-one-year-old visiting my oldest brother, Robert Jr., who had moved years before to take a job on the Ridgecrest/Naval Air Weapons Station (NAWS) China Lake. He and his wife, Mary, worked on the base, and they invited me to live with them at a time when I needed more structure and discipline in my life. They agreed that the change in the environment and the quiet desert life would be just the change I needed. China Lake during the early 1970s was a very quiet town situated about 124 miles east of Los Angeles and about 90 miles west of Bakersfield, California, in the Mojave Desert.

Fighter jets flew out of China Lake on their way to conduct bombing raids in Vietnam. The navy base was the town's biggest employer, and the desert provided extreme heat and a lot of dust storms. This was the town I began to get to know and where I would meet and establish friendly ties with people around my own age. I met Jerry Rodriguez while working a part-time job on the base, which I got with my brother's help. Jerry and I immediately became friends because we liked the same things, such as going places and chasing girls in this little desert town.

On one particular Saturday night, Jerry and I had gone girl chasing for most of the night; Jerry, a Latino of light complexion, had a white girlfriend that he liked and would visit after we had closed the bars down. I am an African American male, with a medium-brown complexion, and would be immediately identified as such. It was a spring night, warm enough that I could stand outside and wait on Jerry when he got out of the car and went into the house to visit his girlfriend.

I got out of the car and walked up to the front door and stood outside the screen door so that if someone slammed it backward hard enough, the door would hit me in the face. I was waiting for Jerry for about twenty minutes when a car pulled up, and three white males jumped out and rushed into the apartment. The leader of the group was more than six feet tall and stoutly built. As he opened the front screen door, he slammed it in my face. As he entered the apartment, I heard him ask Jerry's girlfriend, "Who's that n— standing by the door?"

Most white men know that if you call a black man a n—, more than likely it doesn't matter how large you are or how small he is, you are asking for a physical confrontation.

I waited for him to come out of the building. When he came out, I jumped him and wrapped my arm around his neck in a chokehold.

He was much bigger and stronger than I was. He picked me

up and body slammed me to the ground, but I held on to his neck and landed some solid blows to his head. His two friends were being held back by my friend Jerry, who told them they would not be coming to the aid of their friend, that if they got into the fight he would get into the fight on my side.

As the big guy struggled to get his head out of my headlock, he landed a few blows to the side of my body, but I would not let go and continued slamming my fist into his face as we wrestled on the ground. The fight could have not lasted more than five minutes, and I was relieved when someone yelled, "You guys better stop fighting because the police are coming." I let go of the chokehold, and Jerry and I ran, got into my car, and sped off.

I don't believe my actions in this situation were much different than what would happen today. I would hope Mr. George Zimmerman, in the recent case in Florida, didn't yell at Mr. Trayvon Martin and say, "Hey, n—, what are you doing out here?" But if he did insult Mr. Martin in this manner, my actions show how young black men respond when they are insulted by white men, sometimes without forethought, to their own peril.

"O mankind! We created you from a single (pair) of a male and a female and made you into nations and tribes, that you may know each other (not that you may despise each other). Verily the most honored of you in the sight of G-d is (he who is) the most righteous of you and G-d has full knowledge and is well-acquainted (with all things)"—Quran, 49:13.

1. The Plot: give him an image of a divine savior other than himself, preferably that of a white male

2. The Solution: removal of language and racial imagery that gives divinity to one race at the exclusion of others

If you don't realize your destruction, you will not realize you have a need to be saved.

Chapter 2

The Original Plan

Religious scripture has always played a significant role in the life of all men. Historically it has been a liberating force as well as a force for enslavement. I would like to look at the story of Moses from the Quranic narrative translated by Abdullah Yusuf Ali. We are told that Pharaoh (the king of Egypt) told his soldiers to kill all the male children born to the house of Israel.

From chapter 28 of the Qur'an, Al-Qasas, or The Narration: *In the name of God, Most Gracious, Most Merciful.*

1. Ta. Sin. Mim.
2. These are Verses of the Book that make (things) clear.
3. We rehearse to thee some of the story of Moses and Pharaoh in truth, for people who believe.
4. Truly Pharaoh elated himself in the land and broke up its people into sections, depressing a small group among

them: their sons he slew, but he kept alive their females:
for he was indeed a maker of mischief.

5. And We wished to be Gracious to those who were being
    depressed in the land, to make them leaders (in Faith)
    and make them heirs,

6. To establish a firm place for them in the land, and to show
    Pharaoh, Haman, and their hosts, at their hands, the
    very things against which they were taking precautions.

7. So We sent this inspiration to the mother of Moses:
    "Suckle (thy child), but when thou hast fears about him,
    cast him into the river, but fear not nor grieve: for We
    shall restore him to thee, and We shall make him one of
    Our apostles."

8. Then the people of Pharaoh picked him up (from the
    river): (It was intended) that (Moses) should be to them
    an adversary and a cause of sorrow: for Pharaoh and
    Haman and (all) their hosts were men of sin.

9. The wife of Pharaoh said, "(Here is) joy of the eye, for
    me and for thee: slay him not. It may be that he will be
    of use to us, or we may adopt him as a son." And they
    perceived not (what they were doing)!

10. But there came to be a void in the heart of the mother of
    Moses: She was going almost to disclose his (case), had
    we not strengthened her heart (with faith), so that she
    might remain a (firm) believe,

11. And she said to the sister of (Moses), "Follow him,"
    so she (the sister) watched him in the character of a
    stranger. And they knew not.

12. And we ordained that he refused to suck at first, until
    (His sister came up and) said: "Shall I point out to you

the people of a house that will nourish and bring him up for you and be sincerely attached to him?"

13. Thus We restored him to his mother, that her eye might be comforted, that she might not grieve, and that she might know that the promise of God is true: but most of them do not understand.

14. When he reached full age, and was firmly established (in life), we bestowed on him wisdom and knowledge: for thus do we reward those who do good.

From this narrative, we can see that the help that is being given to Moses comes from G-d, and he also received help from his mother, his sister, and the wife of Pharaoh. This narrative also shows the type of help we get from the important women in our lives. Women can also represent, in scriptural language, a type of womb for the society, a womb that produces humanity with a certain type of individual who is recognizable because of the guidance the womb has given him.

Moses is first delivered from the womb of his mother, and she is inspired by G-d to save her male child from the soldiers of Pharaoh by placing her son in the river. Moses's mother is further inspired by G-d to tell his sister to watch her brother from a distance to see what becomes of his river sojourn. We see in both these episodes that there is a certain amount of care and guidance that these women play in Moses's life, and they are G-d's helpers for the care of Moses. When Moses is taken out of the river, his sister is watching from a distance when she hears him crying. She tells the people who take Moses out of the water that she knows someone who can nurse and take care of him. It was through G-d's grace and intervention that

Moses was given back into the care of his mother. So instead of being destroyed by the command of the ruling power, Moses was saved.

The "destruction of the male child" is an action that is taken in society by those in power to keep a certain segment or type of individual in society from reaching his excellent human potential. Those male individuals are kept out of leadership roles in their personal and family life by those who have the influence of the major institutions in the dominant culture. Historically we have seen this type of game played out by those in power who wish to dominate those males and restrict their power or influence. We should not be deluded into thinking oppression is uniquely a black male or African experience. Throughout recorded history, there has been suppression of the male child without regard to ethnicity. Our historical narrative's observance is not only with the African male child since his arrival on the eastern shores of American as a captured human being under the dominance of white power institutions. We will also seek to examine the damage that has been done to the white male who has bought into the racist ideas of color superiority as being an inherent right or today's prevalent idea of a "privileged white male syndrome."

The African who was brought to the shores of the Americas was whole as a human person upon his departure from his native land. But making him a slave and forcing him to be dominated by another race caused severe damage to his spiritual, moral, physical, and mental well-being. This was done to remake this human being into a totally different person from the one who left his motherland. Slavery was a deliberate and programmed deprivation of withholding education, social structure, and equal work opportunities over a period of decades.

This deprivation produced a human being who was damaged to the essential core of his soul. The essence of any human being is his soul, and when you damage that soul, it takes an act of G-d to restore it back to its original nature. It takes an individual or community of like-minded individuals to recognize that damaged soul and begin the necessary work to restore it back to its noble status, which was created by a merciful and compassionate G-d. His salvation can only come in his individual and community life when he realizes that he was damaged, not with his own or his community's consent but by the design of inhumane institutions and individuals to take away his noble human potential.

These individuals' or institutions' plans were in direct conflict with G-d's plan, which is proclaimed (in Surah al-Qasas 28:5–6), "And we wished to be gracious to those who were being depressed in the land. To make them leaders (in faith) and to make them heirs, to establish a firm place for them in the land, and to show Pharaoh, Haman, and their hosts, at their hands the very things against which they were taking precautions."

By contrast, this inferiority complex, which was meant to do permanent harm to the African male child, has had similar effects on the Caucasian male child. Racial inferiority or superiority is not a healthy mental attitude for any person, and either complex can cause mental and social illness, such as antipathy or apathy.

Those individuals and institutions created a new person not in the image of what G-d wanted but what they wanted.

A demonic or evil-minded person can cause a tremendous amount of damage in those areas man can influence in others, such as his spirit, morals, and physical and mental self. It may take man decades to remake another man into the image he wants, but G-d has only to say, "Be," and it is.

When G-d breathes of his spirit (his knowledge), that man G-d creates is superior to the man society creates. G-d has the power and would not be a just G-d if he witnessed a man (a people) subjected to inhumane treatment by one man (or people) and did not save the man (or people) being mistreated. This is the merciful and compassionate G-d people of faith call on for help when they are oppressed or mistreated.

Chapter 3

How to Destroy the Young Black (or White) Male Child in Thirteen Easy Steps

Step 1: Give him an image of Divine other than himself, preferably that of a white male.

Imam Warith Deen Mohammed is considered one of the great leaders of Islamic thought and human development in the twenty-first century. Imam Mohammed died in 2008, but in the early 1980s, he asked a profound question of the general populous.

"A Message of Concern"
Imam W. Deen Mohammed

What would happen if a people would sit in churches throughout the world for centuries with the image of an African American man as savior of the world before them?

What would this do to the mind of the world's children?"

What would happen to the world's children put under a figure of a particular race presented, pitiable, and in pain "the Savior of all men"?

Qur'an, Surah 3:64:

"Say, oh people of the book. Come to common terms as between us and you: that we worship none but G-d, that we associate no partners with him, that we erect not from among ourselves lords and patrons other than G-d. If then they turn back, say we 'bear witness' that we (at least) are Believers (bowing to G-d's will)."

Civilized nations should want that their religion to be also civilized.

False worship is the worst form of oppression. We are no gods. We are only men. "Mortals from the mortals. He (Allah) created" (Qur'an).

This message of Imam Warith Deen Mohammed shows how a prevalent image of G-d has damaged the soul of all people, but the greatest amount of harm has been done to people of color.

We see in the narrative of the life of Moses that he was brought back into the care of his mother. This is very important because Moses was receiving the loving care and education of his birth mother (society) at the same time he was being educated in the house of Pharaoh. Moses was not culturally or religiously deprived of his native land. To effectively destroy a people or individuals, you need to cut them off from anything that will connect them to their historical past. Moses individually and his people collectively were not destroyed because of this very reason, and they combined their moral and spiritual knowledge with the Egyptians' rational knowledge. Moses was always connected to his people even while he was being raised and educated under the tutelage of Pharaoh.

The destruction of the black male child in America has been just the opposite, and the evidence has been catastrophic for the individuals and their community life development. Whereas Moses was never detached entirely from his family or culture, the African male child arriving on the eastern shores of America was not allowed to make those connections.

The strongest urge the human animal has in his or her life is to know G-d. We have seen throughout evolution man's ability to identify with many animate or inanimate objects that he considers superior to himself. If you give a man an image of G-d only in his own image, this is harmful to him as well as for the one not of that image. The Judeo-Christian scriptures have stated that there should be no graven images made of G-d. This type of worship can be seen in the studies of ancient man. He saw things he considered superior to himself, and his mind couldn't fully comprehend that superiority, so he made those objects gods to worship. This idea of superiority worship of things is alleged to have influenced the ancient Arabs on the Arabian continent to have worshipped more than 360 gods in the Holy City of Mecca. But this was not unique to the ancient Arabs. History is replete with societies that have erected individuals or inanimate objects to be worshipped as gods.

G-d has placed in all human beings the desire to know

him, and when some stray from the path, G-d sends his seers, prophets, and people of spiritual insight to call them back to the worship of one G-d.

That is the reason putting an image of G-d as only a male Caucasian is detrimental to the psyche of all people and to the African male in particular. That image becomes a G-d to be worshiped, feared, and depended upon for his moral, spiritual, and mental salvation. Imam Warith Deen Mohammed has stated why we shouldn't worship mortals: "False worship is the worst form of oppression. We are not gods. We are only men, 'mortals from the mortals, he, Allah, created' (Qur'an)."

A few years ago, prominent Dominican star baseball player Sammy Sosa's facial features started to become whiter and whiter to the extent that it was obvious to the media that this baseball player, with all his wealth and star status, had begun to whiten his facial features surgically or manually. It can be assumed he believed that even with all his money and athletic ability he was still a man of color, and if his dark skin, which G-d gave him, was just a little whiter, he would be a much happier person and be respected by the majority of white folks.

We should ask ourselves, if a person who has reached such a high standing sees himself as inferior because of his color, should we not expect that some persons of color, male and female, young and old, who are marginalized in their financial and social status, would have a similar desire to become white? If we are told that G-d created man in his own image, and that for more than four hundred years the only image you saw of G-d was that of a Caucasian male, it would take a miracle from G-d for you not to want to be white. I am not talking about a miracle from the image makers that we are given of

G-d. I am talking about an inspired message from G-d that is preached from highest levels of the Christian Churches, Jewish Temples, and Masjids (Mosques) by sincere preachers and men and women of G-d who can articulate the message that G-d's image can't be contained in skin color. This message would say that if we want to see G-d in an image, G-d's image first and foremost should be seen in his mercy and compassion; that we belittle G-d when we give him a personality of a certain color and tell people of color around the world that this is their lord and savior and ignore the negative psychological effects this image will produce.

We believe many people who presented this image knew of its harmful psychological effects and promoted this image to control people this image would affect the most, males of color. But the effect was damaged goods in both black and white.

Step 2. Destroy any prominent black male imagery in his history, preferably before that history can become influential in his life.

It has only been in recent American history that any black male has been lifted to a status of historical importance. Most historical depictions of the black male began with the Civil War and that his contribution to American society was that of a slave. The black man who left his mother country was not a slave but a captured human being who would, because of cruel and inhumane treatment to his physical body, eventually capitulate to his captives and become their unwilling servant.

From that day forward, the black male has been under continuous assault, even until this very day with the assault on our President, Mr. Barack Hussein Obama, a

black man of African descent. If someone can denigrate the
president of the United States with obvious racial epitaphs,
we should not be surprised at the destruction of the black
male's character here in America and around the world. The
African male personage can only be elevated to comparable
status with males of other colors when in his own mind
there is self-appreciation for his color. He must know that
his color is something not to be denigrated or marginalized
by him or others.

According to the Qur'an, Surah Fāṭir 35:27–28 (translation
by Yusuf Ali), "Do you not see thou not that God sends
down rain from the sky? With it we then bring out produce
of various colors. And in the mountains are tracts white
and red, of various shades of color, and black intense in
hue. And amongst men and crawling creatures and cattle,
are they of various colors. Those truly fear God, among His
Servants, who have knowledge: for God is exalted in Might,
Oft-Forgiving."

Men, in their plan of racial indignity, may try to supersede
G-d's plan, but G-d's plan encompasses his entire creation with
various colors. None are superior or inferior to the others, and
G-d has the knowledge of all of his creation. Both men and G-d
plan, but G-d is the best planner.

The destruction of the male child has been a phenomenon
in all races, but it has been most evident in the African male
child. Because of the targeted destruction of the male child of
color, we have to examine what has happened to the white male
child. Both have been burdened psychologically by the racial
implication of superiority and inferiority complexes. Both are
damaged goods in black and white.

Step 3. Show him the white female features as the essence of beauty and the black female to be beautiful as long as she has white features.

Historically it has been white men who control the major media outlets that have determined what is considered to be beautiful and what is not. White marketers have told the black male and female that whatever racial features G-d has given him or her are inferior to white features. Society has been told that color, hair, and facial features or any racial identity that is uniquely African is inferior to European. This has caused black women to support this identity of beauty and caused some black men, when given the opportunity, to seek out white women for marriage and companionship. This has been detrimental to the black female's love for her own racial identity and to black female/male relationships.

I am thankful to G-d for blessing me and my brothers with our mother, who was a strong and beautiful black woman. She exemplified the type of woman we should want to marry. My wife and celebrated our Forty third anniversary in July 2016. We met in college, and she exemplified what I wanted in a woman; her black skin and nappy (naturally curly) hair was beautiful because it reminded me of my mother's. G-d has blessed me to be grateful for who I am and not wanting to be someone I am not. G-d has blessed me to see the beauty in our black women, and to remind my five beautiful black daughters of their inherent beauty, which they should embrace wholeheartedly. I would not do what the racists do and put down one race to lift up my own. I am proud of my African heritage and am not ashamed of what G-d has blessed me to be—a human being with that historical perspective and pride, and I don't believe it is racist for other people of other colors or ethnicity to feel likewise; in fact, it would be unhealthy not to.

In a 2012 photo spread, Beyoncé, one of our most popular African American female singers, showed facial coloring that seemed to have been made lighter. It's unfortunate for her as well as for those who gave her the advice that lighter skin would make her more attractive. This particular African American woman has natural looks that don't need anything to improve upon what G-d gave her. Beauty can't be contained in skin color; it can be part of that beauty, and it is impossible for skin color to represent beauty in its entirety. Such an attitude or a belief does damage to the female, black or white, who has this as her frame of reference for beauty. It is also unhealthy for the black or white male child who looks for or relegates beauty only to skin color. The harm can cause psychological, moral, mental, and spiritual harm to any person who primarily sees beauty in skin tone.

Step 4. Give him the idea that his manhood is determined by his ability to run faster, jump higher, and score more points than his white male counterpart, that this is indicative of his superior physical powers and has less to do with intelligence.

I am amazed at the so-called sport analysts who, when analyzing a great athletic play by a black athlete, attribute his ability to athleticism only. These so-called analysts fail to see the intellectual skills of Muhammad Ali when he outsmarted the brute strength of George Foreman or the intellectual mastery and aerodynamic skill of "Dr." Julius Erving with a basketball. We can name many black athletes who played their sports of choice with grace and intellectual astuteness that allowed them to be the best. You can reach only a certain level of athletic ability with strength only. But if you want to achieve a higher level of athletic ability, you must engage your mind to be superior to your opponents.

My mother introduced me to the beauty of boxing with the exceptional punching skills of Joe Louis. Louis didn't take very large swings at his opponents; he had a strong but short jab that he had perfected, a jab that his opponents in the ring, black or white, could not stand up to. This type of skill didn't come from a giant of a man but from one who was intelligent in the science of boxing. Over long periods of time in our country, there has been a conscious effort to explain the great black athlete's skills as something that didn't take intelligence but only natural strength and athletic ability. Unfortunately, some black athletes have drunk some of the "racist Kool-Aid." They see themselves in the same way and do not prepare mentally. I remember years ago hearing how Dick Gregory, who was one of the first African American state winners in Missouri in long-distance races, would use his mind to psych out his opponents in his high-school races.

Black athletes who were at first denied the privilege to compete because of their race measured up to the challenge mentally as well as physically when finally given the opportunity. The racists in sports saw the potential damage to the idea of racial superiority if a white man were to lose the physical and mental battles. Muhammad Ali didn't get the memo, and he out-boxed and outsmarted most of his opponents, black and white. Howard Cosell, a friend and boxing commentator for some of Muhammad Ali's greatest fights, called him a "boxing ring general." All competitive sports require certain degrees of athletic abilities, but the great athletes have the physical prowess and analytical skills of a surgeon.

For some of our greatest black athletes, living and deceased, I submit that some of our historically black colleges, or any college with foresight, should award some of them (posthumously as necessary) a doctor of athletics, or more specifically, DAA degree.

To name a few: Jack Johnson; Walt "The Glyde" Frazier; Willie Mays; Julius Erving; Abdul Kareem Abdul-Jabbar; Michael Jordan; Barry Sanders; Jim Brown; Arthur Ashe; Doug Williams; Lou Brock; Ozzie "The Wizard" Smith; Roberto Clemente; Earl "The Pearl" Monroe; Jessie Owens; Walter "Sweetness" Payton; Paul Robeson; Edwin Moses; Satchel Page; Warren Moon; and Pete "Pistol" Maravich (one of the only white players on the basketball court whose athletic ability, court intelligence, and showmanship were comparable to that of the African American players of his era).

This is only a fraction of great African American athletes past and present who elevated their sport to a higher level with their athletic and intellectual approach. Considering the brutality of the sports, some made unwise decisions to stay in their particular sport too long. Others approached their sport with a mind-set that this sport was a means to an end and not the end within itself. Those individuals walked away from their sport with their body and mind intact.

But we should always be vigilant to counter the racist lies that the black athlete is superior to the white athlete because of his athletic ability, and that a white athlete is superior to a black athlete because of his intellectual ability. Each athlete is gifted by G-d with an inherent physical ability, and there are many other aids he can use to make him a better athlete. The racist ideas of superior and inferior athletic abilities damage the black and white athletes.

Step 5. Give the black woman the idea that she can be both the mother and father of that black male child, and let her think this is her only independent thought.

I am the product of a single black mother who was left with the burden of raising four children on an income of a plantation and migrant labor. Our mother never enjoyed the single life; she was married four times. There are four surnames among my mother's ten children that she gave birth to while married to three of these men. My mother didn't want the burden of trying to raise children without the assistance of their fathers, so she married the men who would become the fathers of her children. She was born in 1913 and was wise and moral enough to want to do what was right for herself and her children.

I was in a conversation with a single black mother recently, who told me that her son never learned to pee standing. He imitated her when he went to the bathroom because she was the first example he saw. Her method was to sit on the toilet, and that was the example he has continued to use to this day into his adulthood.

The idea that any one person can raise a child better than two is a new idea in family life. I have seen the results of single women trying to raise a male child on their own. The results have been one of two outcomes: either the male child becomes a "momma's boy," or he becomes an incorrigible child who has to be disciplined by legal authorities. Unless the male child is fortunate enough to have a person of parental influence (PI), someone who takes the interest of that of a parent and guides that child toward good choices in life, that child will suffer from the lack of parental support and parental guidance a two-parent house generally offers.

I am the father of five daughters and the brother of five sisters, and I have seen the damage my nephews have suffered because of an absentee father. I don't want that for my daughters. There is something to the adage that "a boy can make a baby, but it takes a man to be a father." We should applaud those single women who are left to raise those male children on their own. However, we should also demand of our sons that if they are man enough to father a child, they should be man enough to take care of that child.

Step 6. Make educational pursuits hard but crime and sport and play easy for the black male child.

Statistically, the chances that a young black man will have a criminal record are greater than his having a having a high-school diploma. This is a sad commentary about our society and how we treat our young black men. An older black gentleman recently told me something startling. He said that when he was growing up in the city of St. Louis, black men who were stopped by a white policeman would be questioned whether they had a criminal record or not. If they said they didn't have a record, the arresting white officer would respond by saying, "Well, you got one now," and proceed to arrest the young black man. This now older black gentleman told me that when he was stopped by a white policeman and asked if he had a criminal record, he would always respond yes. Unfortunately, this type of racial profiling and pushing young black males toward criminal behavior is something that has only recently become a matter of open discussion.

I have an experience I would like to share. In the early part of the 1970s, I was a young activist who was involved in a committee to raise money for legal funds for political activists who were in jail or on trial for their antigovernment activities. A person who was later identified as a government informant tried to persuade me and another young activist to rob a bank. We found out after his death that he was working with the local and federal authorities to set us up to commit a crime. I am to this day glad my mother didn't raise her son to be someone who wanted to do wrong but one who saw what he perceived as a wrong and would try to do his part in making it right. This happened to me, and I am sure there are many black men who are dead or incarcerated because of schemes on their lives by others who didn't value their humanity because of their skin color.

I was a chaplain at Menard State Prison in Chester, Illinois, when then governor George Ryan placed a moratorium on death sentences of all inmates on death row. I had the opportunity to meet some of those inmates whose sentences would be overturned by the courts for lack of credible evidence when closer scrutiny was made. The moratorium, which Governor Ryan initially placed on the execution of these inmates, would eventually lead to those sentences being commuted to life without the possibility of parole.

Because of the efforts of some students and the deliberate guidance of some concerned professors at one of our most prestigious Midwest universities, the lives of some innocent young men of color were spared. Those of us who have interacted with some of these young men celebrate with them and applaud the diligent efforts of all of those people who, with G-d's grace, were able to right a wrong that would have taken the lives of some innocent men.

My wife and I are the parents of seven children, five girls and two boys. We (and the whole nation) witnessed the tragic murder of more than twenty innocent children and six adult faculty members in Sandy Hook Elementary School by a young man who had access to his mother's guns. As parents, we must always try to be the influence that will have the greatest positive impact on our children's lives.

When our sons were growing up, my wife and I would never allow them to play with water guns. My wife still has all the toy water guns our children's grandparents and other family members gave them; those guns are hidden in drawers in our bedroom. My wife never let our kids play with them because of her fear of the message they might give our two sons. Instead, she and I took them to baseball practice and little league games. They both played high-school sports, and we supported them on that level of activity. They turned out to be excellent young men who are college graduates; both have served as naval officers on submarines. One is still active, and the other is on active reserve. We made a choice not to let sports become the biggest influence in their lives and to make educational excellence a goal to pursue. We are proud of both our sons who graduated from high school and college with honors. As parents, we made the decision to make educational pursuit easy and the pursuit of crime hard. We invite you to do the same.

Step 7. Take away as many legal success opportunities from him as possible, and make illegal ones easy to become involved in.

There is a strong belief among some African Americans that drugs and firearms are brought (some say dumped) into the predominantly African American communities by someone other than the communities' residents to make them easy to obtain. This idea may be an urban legend, but the concern about the infiltration of drugs and guns needs to have a source that can be explained, and so far none has been found.

I was told by a person in law enforcement that some drug dealers in African American communities were allowed to deal drugs there longer so as to build a bigger case against them when they would eventually be arrested on drug-dealing charges. This cavalier attitude by law enforcement authorities is known by the youths in these communities, and some of them try to earn a living selling drugs. Unfortunately for these youths, the math does not add up: they are usually given longer sentences because of the longer observation by law enforcement authorities. The idea for longer sentences for drug selling and use is known as the Rockefeller Rule. It was named after the mayor of New York who, after his city experienced a high rate of crime due to drug use and trafficking in the 1980s, initiated longer sentences for those involved in drug use and distribution.

I have a friend who is a graduate of a technical high school here in our city that has long been closed. It is his belief, and the belief of many other African American residents in the city, that the technical high school was closed because of the equal opportunities young black men were getting to compete for union jobs in the trades after graduation with craftsman skills.

Whatever our beliefs, statistics will prove whether they have any basis for concern. The facts are that we make up only approximately 12 percent of the population, but as an ethnic group, black males make up more than 65 percent of the prison population in some prisons. This is not an accident; we can see evidence of unequal sentencing in the possession and distribution of certain drugs based on race. This sentencing inequity has been addressed to some extent, but it is not equal as of this writing (fall 2014) for everyone: black, white, and brown.

This balance between available illegal drug and the lack of equal job opportunities has produced damaged goods in black and white.

Step 8. Make games of chance, prostitutions, drugs, and illegal weapons easy to obtain.

I was working in my backyard several years ago, digging a hole large enough for a man to get into in order to replace a broken sewer line. I had dug about six feet long and two feet wide when a young lady came into my backyard where I was working with a laborer. All of a sudden, she jumped into the hole, raised her panty-less skirt, and asked me to have sex with her. I asked her to lower her skirt and to get out of my way because I had work to do, and it didn't involve working with her. In some neighborhoods, prostitution is allowed to exist openly and without any discouragement from law enforcement, and it continues as business as usual.

Games of chance and the number games used to be played

behind closed doors in poor African American communities. Now they are out in the open. Casinos and lottery games continue to be an easy sell in African American and other poor communities across America. Poverty has a tendency to make those people directly affected by it to be more optimistic about their chances to be that one in a million to win. St. Louis, the city where I currently reside, is surrounded by casino boats. You can find a casino conveniently located on every major freeway.

In the 1980s, when we were at the height of the crack epidemic in our neighborhood, I was interviewed by NPR (National Public Radio) because of my community involvement and my desire to try to restore some of the older abandoned homes as investment properties. The young lady who interviewed me came over as it was getting dark, and she could hear gunshots. She asked with disbelief what all that shooting was about. I responded that it was young drug dealers warring with each other. During those years, gunfire was routine when it grew dark. My wife and I would try to speak with as many of the young gang members or drug dealers as we could. We would suggest that rehabbing some of these older homes was much more profitable than drugs and a lot less hazardous to their health. Also, we would inform them that we would call the police whenever we saw them involved in drug sales.

They would say, "Mr. Wali, are you going to call the police on us?"

I would say, "Son, you are doing something illegal. When you stop selling drugs, I'll stop calling the police."

My wife and I were asleep early one fall morning when we were suddenly woken by rapid gunfire, which seemed to be close to our home. We immediately heard loud screams coming from the gangway between our home and the home next door. I rushed downstairs and ran outside to find a young man who had been shot in the leg, begging me not to let whoever was chasing him kill him. I assured the young man I would not let anyone kill him and yelled upstairs for my wife to call 911. We were able to get him the required help, and he survived. I saw him sometime later, and he had left the gang. He was smart enough to learn from this incident.

Throughout this period of the late 1980s and the '90s, America had a war on drugs, and our young black men were having wars amongst themselves. There were so many casualties in the black communities during this time in America; it appeared those young black men who were not killing each other were being sentenced to long prisons terms in an unjust legal system.

Prostitutions, drugs, guns, and games of chance have always been easy to sell or obtain in black communities. Most of these illegal acts have been influenced directly or supported by persons from outside the black communities for their own financial gains. Most people with bad intentions know there is money to be made off the poor and destitute.

What makes these illegal acts pervasive and seemingly unstoppable is the silence of those who suffer the most from these acts: those people who live in the neighborhoods where these acts occur. Our faith and our fears are tested in our neighborhoods with these illegal acts, and our fear seems to be the constant winner. I believe if our faith were stronger than our fears, we could leave some of our houses of worship, which are on most corners in our neighborhoods, and go speak to our sons, daughters, friends, and neighbors about their acts, which make our neighborhoods fertile grounds for these crimes. Although others help in the proliferation of prostitution, drugs, guns, and games of chance, we who are residents of these communities have a responsibility to speak and act forcefully to those who would continue to weaken the moral fabric of our communities.

When immoral and illegal behavior is allowed to go unabated in one community, it is only karma that it will also eventually affect those individuals from the protected community who would like to test the waters of immorality. We have to consider that those things that are prohibited could have a lure for individuals who would like to take a bite out of the forbidden fruit. Vibrant and healthy communities should be a concern of all people of goodwill. All should help prevent damaged goods in black and white.

Step 9. Let him think there is nothing wrong with doing time in prison because his father, mother, and some of his friends have done time and that somehow gives him credibility in his neighborhood.

About twenty years ago, at the height of the crack epidemic in our neighborhood, I had an opportunity to talk with several young African American men about their involvement in selling drugs. I explained that an alternate opportunity to buy and sell distressed properties was a lot less dangerous and much more profitable. I suggested selling drugs would limit their options to two possibilities: incarceration or death. They stated that they didn't mind going to jail, that they probably would be incarcerated with some of their friends. They didn't address the possibility of death, and ignoring this was a mistake on their part. Of the three young men I talked to in those days, two were killed by gun violence; the third young man was saved when his mother moved with him out of the neighborhood.

I have spent approximately thirty-five years working and volunteering in the prisons of Missouri and Illinois, and I never meet anyone who will admit that he enjoyed his time while incarcerated. Most of these men told me they were looking forward to leaving prison, and most swore to G-d they would never come back. I have one friend who said they would have to kill him before he would allow someone to send him back to prison.

Prison life affects the total being, during and after his time of incarceration. The total environment can cause an immediate impact on the inmate upon his arrival to prison. While I was a chaplain in one of Illinois's prisons, I had the opportunity to talk with a new inmate who upon his arrival went on a hunger strike to seek his release. I advised him to eat because his hunger strike would not get him released. He told me his plan was to remain on his hunger strike and that he was going to stay with it. He stayed with his plan, and unfortunately, after going without food for such a long period, his body shut down, and he eventually died from his hunger strike. He left the prison—but not the way he wanted to.

I was doing my visits to the cell blocks one day when one of the prison guards opened a cell to put an inmate in with an inmate who was presently living in the cell alone. The inmate who was living in the cell told the guard, "I told you I will kill this man if you put him in this cell with me, and if you leave him with me he will be a dead man." This was an inmate telling the guard his intention to kill his soon-to-be cellmate to his face. Although the guard had a job to do, he gave in to the inmate's request, realizing that to do otherwise might end in the death of the second inmate.

Prison guards have some of the most stressful and dangerous jobs a person can have. Most individuals who say that they don't mind doing time are talking about the city jails, not state or federal prisons. Doing twenty-four or forty-eight hours in a city or county jail is not the same as doing time in a state or federal prison. The mind-set of the individual changes when he walks into a state or federal prison and realizes that he is going to be incarcerated for a long time.

In my many conversations with inmates with long prison sentences, I had the opportunity to meet a man who was celebrating his forty-second birthday in prison. He told me that he'd been sentenced to fifty years without parole when he was seventeen years old. So he was celebrating his forty-second birthday in prison, and he had done twenty-five years of a fifty-year sentence and had twenty-five more years to do before his sentence would be done. He told me that when he was sentenced by the judge in the courtroom that day at age seventeen, it was like a big explosion of light went off in his brain, and that explosion helped him maintain his sanity for all the twenty-five years of his confinement. He told me he had tried Christianity, Al-Islam, and other religions, but the only thing that had helped keep him G-d conscious and sane of mind was that explosion that went off in his brain. Being a person of faith, I could not ask him to give up a belief that he perceived as the source that had kept him G-d conscious and sane in an environment that can cause many men to go insane and become faithless.

Because of my work as a chaplain at Menard State Prison in Chester, Illinois, I was privy to learn that the rate of recidivism for inmates in the prison system in Illinois had a strong correlation to religious service attendance. Those inmates who attended religious services four or more times per month or on a regular basis were less likely to be recycled back into the Illinois prison system than those inmates who attended religious services fewer than four or more times monthly, or not at all. Regular religious attendance was a better indicator of the rate of recidivism than having job skills after prison or educational pursuits while confined in prison. But the chaplaincy and other religious services in the Illinois prison system have been dramatically cut back. I have witnessed firsthand the cuts in religious services.

Parents shouldn't let their children grow up to have a cavalier attitude about prison life or doing prison time. The personalities of those who work in or who are incarcerated in the prison system are affected in ways that are life-altering. Some changes will be for the better and some will be for the worse, but the prison environment will change their lives.

Step 10. Let him think he has to get rich quick or die trying because he will not live to become thirty years old, and let him think this is his own independent thought.

I have a neighbor who told me that when her son was three, he told her he didn't think that he would live to be thirty. I told her this wasn't an independent thought of a three-year-old because most three-year-olds can't count to thirty, and that he must have heard it from an older person or on some radio or TV program. She also told me that as he grew to become a young man of nineteen, he repeated this thought, saying he didn't believe he would live to reach thirty. He was right. My neighbor told me that another young African American male shot and killed her son less than a block away from his home when he was just twenty-four.

We have to be very conscious of what we accept as our own mind's ideas that are not our own, and not let other people's evil thoughts become our own.

The idea of trying to get rich quick is counterintuitive to investing for long-term success, not only success for ourselves during our lifetimes but to enjoy our success during our retirement years and also to ensure that future generations of our children and grandchildren may enjoy the fruits of our righteous labor. We should never be content just to think of our own financial success and enjoyment during our lifetime without showing an interest in the financial and social heath of family and friends and the philanthropic well-being of others after our life on earth.

This idea of dying young is one that has caused havoc in poor and minority communities because youths in these communities seem to be most affected by this notion. We find that these youths are most interested in defending drug turfs as territories for making quick cash off their own communities in illegal drug sales. This has become the premiere job description for the get-rich-quick-or-die-trying scheme. The hip-hop culture has been influenced by former drug dealers who used their experiences in selling or using drugs to popularize or legitimize this scheme.

The number of young men, mostly from poor and minority communities, who have died of gun violence because of their drug involvement in the past thirty years is estimated to be in the tens of thousands.

The drug market is a major contributor to the nation's homicide rate. Indeed, the peak in homicides during the mid-1980s was directly related to the saturation of urban areas with the crack cocaine drug trade. Methamphetamine—more powerful, more addictive, and easier to produce than crack cocaine—is becoming a major drug of choice in urban, suburban, and rural communities. If the methamphetamine trade results in drug wars on the same scale as those of the 1980s, it is possible that homicide rates will begin to climb once more, as drug dealers are among those most likely to carry weapons.

Gangs have proliferated rapidly since 1980, when there were about 2,000 gangs with 100,000 members in 286 cities.[1] By 1996, there were 31,000 gangs with 846,000 members in 4,800 cities and towns.[2]

Gangs are more likely to recruit adolescents who own firearms, and gang members (who are twice more likely to own guns for protection than non-gang members) are more likely to carry guns outside their homes.[3] The risk of being killed is sixty times greater among young gang members than in the general population[4] and in some cities far higher. For example, the St. Louis youth gang homicide rate is a thousand times higher than the US homicide rate.[5]

Although not all gangs are drug organizations, gang membership appears to increase individual participation in drug use and trafficking, gun carrying, violence, and prolonged involvement in drug sales.[6] Furthermore, gang activity is no longer a problem that is unique to urban communities. From 1989 to 1995, the percentage of students who reported that street gangs were present at school increased by 186 percent in suburban schools and 250 percent in rural schools. Gangs reportedly operate in 41 percent of urban schools, 26 percent of suburban schools, and 20 percent of rural schools. Long-term solutions to address the problem of gun violence must include a comprehensive approach to reducing the number of youth involved in gangs.

We have to address the problem of our youths and their infatuation with "pop culture" as parents, and as a society who sees the investment that we get from directing our youth to what is in their best interest individually, and to that of the community in which they live. We can begin this investment with one parent at a time. We need to know where our children are but also to let them know that certain influences in their lives are tantamount to a death sentence or, at the minimum, incarceration.

Step 11. Let him think it is better to be a "player" (not responsible) than a father or husband.

From the marriage relationship, children are born into a family unit. This is what makes a healthy and vibrant community. To be responsible and present in the lives of the children that you have fathered provides social and financial stability to the family. In the African American communities, the legacy of slavery didn't support the ideas of family life for the slaves on the plantations. But as men who are descendents of that peculiar and wretched period of our country's history, we have to recognize that we can no longer use that legacy of slavery as an excuse to engage in behavior that does not support family life.

Our communities are weakened when fathers are absent and when they don't take on the responsibilities as guardians and protectors of their families. We can't blame other races or men for our lack of family backbone. Before you decide to become a father, you should know you are ready to take on the responsibility of fatherhood. If you are not ready to take on the financial and social responsibility that calls for, you should take all necessary precautions to prevent unplanned pregnancies. I am the great-uncle of many grandnieces and grandnephews whose fathers unfortunately went after the sexual pleasure but forgot the responsibilities that come with it if children are the result.

Fathers should be adamant about the need to be proactive in matters of planning to become a father. Fatherhood should not be an accident, and it definitely shouldn't be a matter that you are in doubt about: whether you are the father or need a DNA test. The legacy of community life is fostered and developed from strong family life. Where you find dysfunctional and broken families, you will find neighborhoods that are dysfunctional and broken down.

This is not a blanket statement that every family in a dysfunctional neighborhood is dysfunctional. But in the instances where they are not dysfunctional, we know that present in those households are individuals and families who hold onto faith in G-d and seek to guide and direct their children toward what is right. We know a strong community life supports a strong family, and a strong family life supports a strong community life. However, it is up to the fathers to take a robust and strong stand on being the leaders and protectors of their families and for the best interest of the community. We can no longer be absentee fathers in our children's lives.

Not to digress but to make a point: some other races see the need for the father to remain present in their children's lives. I am a fan of the "Dear Abby" advice column and have been reading it for many years. Years ago I read a letter from a father who came home and found his wife having sex with a man on his couch. This father related to "Dear Abby" that he and his wife had two young sons whom he loved dearly. The father stated that he was very hurt to witness his wife's lack of control of her sexual urges and her disrespect for their family. However, he stated that he would remain in the home with his two sons to protect them and to be that father figure when needed. But he also stated that when his two sons became grown and left home, he would then reevaluate his relationship with his wife as to whether to remain in the marriage or to seek a divorce. This father placed the welfare and guidance that he could provide for his sons over the hurt and pain his wife caused him in her lack of moral fortitude. This is the attitude we need to have if we are to make our family and community life stronger. As fathers, we should be willing to sacrifice some of our personal wants and needs for what is best for the wholesome growth and development of our community and family life.

Community life is the key, and we should all be consistent in promoting healthy family life as being the foundation for healthy community life. We as fathers should be front and center in leading the charge and being the standard bearers for supporting healthy community life.

Step 12. Show him successful black men who were ex-drug dealers or wannabe drug dealers who are now giants in the movie and music industries, and make it seem easy for him to follow that model.

Our young man of color and, to a lesser degree, poor men of all races, have been used as tools of the powerful elite in the film and the music industries. These men who determine what is and is not promoted to the general public. They use their wealth and the ability to make or break film- or movie-star wannabes, forcing them to act the way they want the masses to see or hear.

I watched a movie several years ago where one of our most talented and beautiful black actresses starred in a role that was degrading to her and to the legacy of other black actresses who had made it possible for her to achieve her status in the movie industry. This degrading and repugnant role won Halle Berry an Academy Award. I suggest if you look through the archives of the history of filmmaking in this country, you would not find a white actress asked to perform such a degrading sex scene for a major movie network that would be made available for the general public viewing without a triple-X rating.

Is reality TV real? There are several African American male actors who have, with the help of powerful men in the movie industry, parlayed their drug and gang affiliation into movies and reality TV shows. One of our most acclaimed African American singers, Whitney Houston, was cast along with her husband, Bobby Brown, in a very degrading and insulting role on so-called reality TV.

The only thing real about these shows is the lack of respect these individuals have for themselves and how little respect the people responsible for putting on these shows have for the actors and the audience. It shows utter disrespect for those people of color who are cast in demeaning roles that degrade their inherent human nobility. This is done by powerful people in the film and recording industries to dehumanize people of color and to show the world that as a people, we don't have to be respected. These powerful people believe that as persons of color we will accept any demeaning or insulting role we can get to have our face or voice heard or seen by others. Today we can make decisions that would not only benefit those individuals who want to be players in the entertainment industry but who refuse to sell their souls and dignity for that opportunity. We can and should say to those who would ask us to demean ourselves and our race that we may lose some financial gain, but we refuse to be cast in roles that insult our dignity.

Step 13. Promote negative imagery of men of color—of black men in particular—at all costs. But if there should ever be one who rises up and has the audacity to not let his color define his intelligence or human worth, let the full force of racial superiority rise to destroy this model because this model should be kept invisible and nonexistent.

I recently read a story about an advertisement that appeared on some mass transit busses in a major city on the West Coast. The ad was underwritten by the FBI and the advertisement suggested the face of terrorism belonged to a man of Arab descent. After vigorous complaints of racial profiling and stereotyping, an apology was issued by the FBI and the advertisement was eventually removed.

As a nation, state, or city, we can't let a vocal minority, or those who wish to define people of color in ways they perceive them, set the vision for the community at large. In the city where I reside there is an ongoing lawsuit in one county municipality where it was alleged that one of the commanding officers of this police department asked its predominately white officers to harass and arrest young black men who would frequent the malls in their district. Fortunately, to their credit and their humanity, none of the officers followed through on their commanding officer's orders, and, furthermore, reported him to his superiors. Everyone thereof humanity. We have to judge each person as an individual soul.

Two recent incidents that happened to our presidents give us a perception of disrespect for their political leadership. George W. Bush traveled abroad to a Muslim country during the latter part of his second term; as he was being questioned during a news conference, one of the participants took off one of his shoes and threw it at the president. He was able to duck and not be hit by the shoe. We are told that in Muslim countries, this act of throwing a shoe at someone is a grave insult.

In the second case, President Barack Obama was giving a State of the Union annual report when a Caucasian congressman in the gallery yelled out during one of his remarks, calling the president a liar. This is not normal protocol and shows a tremendous lack of respect by the congressman for himself and for the office of the president, particularly for the man who is presently occupying that office.

In the first instance, President Bush was attacked for his political policies as they affected Muslim countries. In the second instance, President Obama was attacked for his color and not for his political policies. We have witnessed a high degree of disrespect for the office and for the man who now occupies that office, a man who happens to be of African descent. Some Caucasians have shown through their actions that they still haven't fully come to realize that this black man is the commander-in-chief of the most influential nation in the world, and G-d willing, he will continue to be commander-in-chief despite their refusal to believe this has actually happened during their lifetime. He will, with G-d's protection, complete his second term in office and leave the office of president of the United States of America with a legacy for people of color and others the world over to respect and appreciate.

Chapter 4

How to Save the Male Child (with Special Emphasis on the Male Child of African Descent) in Thirteen Easy Steps

Step 1. To be human and proud is more important than to be black, brown, yellow, or white and proud.

The perception you have of yourself is more important than the perception others may have of you. Your racial identity does not magnify your humanity. G-d has created you with a nobility inherent in your original nature. You only lose that nobility through the acts and plans of diabolical forces who know what G-d's aim is for your inherent growth and development. Those diabolical forces then intercede in G-d's plan and give you a destructive plan that causes you to wander in darkness and self-destruction. Help comes to those lost souls when G-d sends someone to intercede on their behalf with G-d's light and guidance.

We must guide our young men to understand that their destiny is similar to everything else in creation and that G-d is the finality. This life is but play and amusement, and we should enjoy the good things in life, but we should not forget that our life is but a test, and our real destiny is the life after this life. Our life is similar to that of a plant in that its initial development is hidden from our sight, but we see it sprout and blossom into a beautiful plant, and we enjoy the fruit it bears and grows and is admired by everyone who sees it.

But soon that plant, which at one time was tall and strong, now seems to be withering away, and soon that the plant has died. This is the similarity of our life to that of a plant. Although the plant can't plan its life, we can plan ours. As parents and guardians of our young men, let us all be instruments in building healthy and wholesome lives for our young men. Our failure to not help in the planning of our sons' futures means others take over with nefarious (criminal) plans for our sons.

Step 2. Give him moral, spiritual, and socially conscious images to imitate.

Begin with yourself. Cultivate a strong concern for others. We can't ignore our own well-being, but we should realize that the concern for family and community supersedes the individual concern. My individual concerns for strong morals should be strong enough to witness in my family and in my community life. Spiritual involvement in a religious organization or with a group of like-minded spiritual individuals should be something I actively participate in and encourage others to do. To want for my fellow human being what I want for myself should be evidenced in my works, and we should be exemplary in our community as persons of good moral character. We should want to be excellent role models in the home that our sons can emulate.

When our eldest son graduated from high school, he was honored as a scholar athlete by the city's daily newspaper. The reporter who was doing the story on scholar athletes asked my son who his role model was, and my son replied it was his father. Whether we realize it or not, our children will imitate their parents and will pick up their nuances and habits, good or bad, sometimes consciously and sometimes unconsciously, so we have to be very careful of what we say and do in front of our children.

In my job as a prison chaplain, one of my duties was to visit the inmates in the different buildings where they were housed. This particular prison in southern Illinois had approximately thirty-five hundred inmates. One day, one of the inmates said to me, "Wali, today is my son's birthday."

I said, "Congratulations. How old is he?"

He told me his age, and then I asked him where he lived. He told me he was on the gallery above him and asked if I would go up there and wish him a happy birthday for him. I told him in a not-so-polite way that I would not wish his son a happy birthday because I didn't see anything happy about a father and son celebrating a birthday together in prison.

Our sons observe their first role models in the men or women in their home or community, and they will emulate those individuals whose influence—positive or negative— they respect the most.

Step 3. Reinforce the need to read and put into his immediate living environment positive religious and

historical bibliographies, or any reading materials that will enlighten his thinking in a positive way.

Reading enriches the mind for growth and exploration of places and things others have seen or done. These places and experiences can be the impetus for a developing mind to say, "I can actualize my belief that I can become a doctor, lawyer, teacher, scientist," or any professional occupation. We should be trying to influence our young men to see that they are becoming positive role models in their own lives. We see in the scriptures of the Bible of the Christians and the Quran of the Muslims the importance of reading. The Christians' Bible says in the Gospel of John that "in the beginning was the Word, and the word was G-d and the word moved on the face of the earth." Those of us of the Christian faith know that for us to get to know G-d we must read our book, the Bible, and pray that G-d blesses us with understanding of the words we read in the Bible. The admonition to read "the Word" was the first revelation given to those of us who seek to know G-d and to follow the guidance he wants in our lives.

The Muslims' book of guidance is called the Quran, and the first revelation that was given to them was to "read." Chapter 96 states, "Read in the name of your Lord and Cherisher, who created, Created man out of clot of congealed blood, read, and your lord is most Bountiful." For those of us who follow the Islamic faith, we know for us to get to know G-d and to follow his guidance that we must "read" our book, the Quran, and ask G-d to increase our knowledge of the Quran. We as people of faith should have a habit of reading the Bible, the Quran, and any other spiritual or religious books that direct us to a better understanding of the Creator.

We can all see the importance of "reading" when two of the major faith groups have invited their followers to adhere to "reading."

Reading should be required of our sons, and they should have ample positive reading materials to interest them. Making the Holy Bible and the Holy Quran available would be a benefit for religious and moral guidance for all our youths. The Gideons must had some divine intuition when they started making the Holy Bible available to travelers in motels and other places of rest to ensure that if travelers needed to read, the word of G-d would always be conveniently available. This idea is a good one for our homes.

My close friend Rashid Shabazz lives in Las Vegas, Nevada, and he told me something recently that I had not been told by anyone, black or white. Rashid, who is now a young fifty-eight-year-old independent businessman, said that as an eighteen-year-old African American male, he realized that he would have to compete in a world that demanded literacy. To be competitive in any business, he would have to be as informed as his competition, and this information was available in books. He would need to increase his reading and study habits more on current and established authors whose writings would enlighten his young but inquisitive business mind. He made the decision to read eight hours a day to make sure he was abreast of current events and informed on positive business ideas that would help him become a better and more informed businessman. He said that in his forty years of study, he has read hundred of books that have been invaluable to his success as a businessman. To invite our young men to make a lifelong habit of reading would make their lives more informed and rewarding.

Another friend, Jeffery Crumer, is a sport historian on players' names, individual statistics, teams they played for, and a lot of information who can impress others with his knowledge on sports in the past three decades. When you ask him how he became so informed, he says he reads the sport page eight to ten minutes a day. Those of us who enjoy sports know if we have a sports question we need the correct answer to, we can call on Jeff. I am sure if he wanted to, he could host a call-in sports talk show.

Your son may not see himself reading for eight hours daily, but it would be a rewarding experience educationally if he would allow himself eight to ten minutes daily to read something positive. It would be helpful if parents would provide those materials for their sons in their homes. My daughter, who is a speech therapist and has her master's degree from one of the premier universities here in St. Louis, reminded me recently how her mother and I made sure our children had plenty of positive reading materials to read when they were younger. Reading is the first step toward a more informed life. "If you can't read, you can't lead."

Step 4. Tell him to revere the womb that produced him and all women—his mother, grandmother, aunts, and the community—who nourished and influenced his life.

We have too many young black males who sing about the love of their mothers in their songs, while at the same time their behavior toward other women of color would cause you to question their sincerity. Behavior toward one's mother should be of love and reverence, and the same love and reverence should be shown toward all women. Men who are fathers of daughters only want their daughters to be in relationships with men whom they feel will not harm their daughters physically or psychologically. Fathers should be exemplary in front of their sons when talking to their mothers or daughters, and they should never be physically or psychologically abusive to women in or out of the presence of their sons.

We never want to be the negative example our sons reference as the reason they are abusive to their spouses or girlfriends. A father is the first teacher about how to treat the women he loves, especially the mother of his children. Our son will either be a man who respects his wife as his father respected his mother, or he will abuse his wife the same way his father abused his mother. As fathers, we should want to be the best example of a husband, protector, and provider for our family our sons can witness. As a father, I hope and pray my sons can say this about me.

Step 5. Advise him to respect himself if he wants others to respect him.

My mother loved music of all kinds, but she was especially fond of the Staple Singers and their hit, "Respect Yourself." She loved it both for its tune and its message. The theme was that if you want other people to respect you, you'd better respect yourself first. The human creature can be the noblest of creatures, or he can be the worst of G-d's creatures. He can choose to be respectful of himself and others, or he can choose to be a person who is disrespectful of himself and others.

We have to remind our sons through our own actions and deeds toward others the type of character they should want to personify. Remind them that respect is something that is not only earned but can be and probably should be given freely. A person may do something that may cause you to disrespect his or her actions, but you should always respect the essence of his or her humanity. Our human self can be, G-d willing, resurrected from the depth of sinful and shameful acts. But it will only happen when you realize you must respect your human essence in yourself and others. We have to cherish and protect that human nobility. We should never disrespect the human potential for excellence in ourselves and others.

Step 6. The mind is infinite; the body is definite. Make greater use of the mind for perpetuity.

"Man means mind." Imam Warith Deen Mohammed, one of the foremost Islamic scholars of the twenty-first century, made this statement approximately three decades ago. But in the community of men of color, this is not what we have visualized a man to be. We have been told and have to a large degree accepted the idea of a man as being a "white or Caucasian male."

We see the Caucasian male as the model for our maleness. If we are to take our rightful place in the universe of humanity of men, we must begin to see that G-d has given all men and women the same mind of unlimited potential. We need to see G-d not as an image of a Caucasian man but as the creator of the heavens and the earth and everything between these two bodies. Our mind's potential is not limited by what others may say our intellectual potential is.

Racists have used color and place of original birth as indicators of mental capacity. The man who recognizes that G-d cannot be pictured or visualized has expanded his mind to the potential of unlimited spiritual and mental growth. G-d is not limited in his ability to give his wisdom or inspiration to anyone he chooses, but G-d will not inspire a mind that has limited G-d as a physical entity. G-d is greater and infinite and cannot be visualized. We should realize we only limit our own mental potential when we limit G-d's capacity to a physical entity. Our minds are too small to visualize the universe and its unlimited resources. But our minds can take us to the point of the "black hole" in the universe where our minds are not limited to space or time.

Step 7. Lifelong education is not an option but a reality.

We should always encourage our young men of color and be exemplary in our own lives as someone with a lifelong desire to learn. The mind will continue to function at a very high level of normalcy as long as that mind is exercised in a way to keep it alert. There is no way better than to keep the mind alert than to read. Reading exercises the brain in the same manner that swimming exercises the body. An active brain will stay alert and functional when it is exercised, just as the body will stay alert and functional as long as it is exercised.

Reading materials that support healthy moral and spiritual attitudes in one's thoughts are the vitamins that keep the brain healthy. We should recommend to our youth reading materials that will support an appreciation for what is just and moral. We should instill in them a desire to educate themselves wherever the opportunity presents itself. Once a mind is educated to the freedom that reading gives, it is practically impossible to limit that mind for growth.

Step 8. Make crime objectionable and not an option in his life.

Don't condone any element of crime. When our youngest son was about fourteen, one day he wanted to wear to school a bandana representing the colors of the "Bloods." I took that bandana from him and told him that any type of gang support or indication of affiliation would not be tolerated in our house and he would not leave our home with that bandana on his head. Both our sons are military officers today, but when they were growing up, my wife didn't allow them to play with water guns or any guns. Today, both have served our nation as nuclear submarine officers. I don't think their mother harmed them in the least by not allowing them to play with guns when they were growing up.

We can't give our sons or daughters the idea that we will support or condone criminal or immoral behavior in our homes. The home should be a place where we teach our children the type of responsible adult behavior that we want them to exhibit in society. When we see in our sons or daughters attitudes or behaviors that we find objectionable to our own conscience or moral standards, we should immediately try to stop it before it becomes unstoppable.

Step 9. Don't make gambling or drug or alcohol usage a way to ignore the reality of the present situation and not look for a permanent solution to the problem.

The destruction of an individual, a community, or a nation can be initiated through gambling and drug or alcohol abuse, but when an individual or community is subjected to these influences, it is like having a losing trifecta. Those of us who know this must protect our young men from the influences that can handicap their futures. We must explain and be exemplary in our own lives that we will not damage our present situation or environment with games of chance or alcohol or drug abuse.

We must make a concerted effort to alleviate obstacles and challenges in our lives with faith in G-d and a determined spirit to do good for ourselves and others. We must insist that our young men of color understand that their problems will not be solved by others. Our sons must see that others may not see their concerns as of interest to them. His competition may not be his neighbor next door but someone in another country. To indulge in unhealthy habits will only make him less competitive in the global market of goods and services. We must give our young men the building blocks in life that will give them an opportunity for success. We should tell them to worship G-d as the creator of the heavens and the earth, and to know that G-d is aware of all their deeds, good or bad, and they will be rewarded by G-d accordingly.

Step 10. Saving money and having a consistent work habit for himself or others are proven tools for a successful economic life.

Work is not a "four-letter word" but an indicator of life and social development. To have a healthy social life, we need to make contributions to our own financial welfare. I am a big proponent of entrepreneurship or self-employment initiatives. I am not opposed to being employed by others, but you can provide more income for yourself and your family if you find a product or service in which you can become proficient enough to offer to the general public. When you employ yourself, your income is not dependent on what someone may determine your hourly, weekly, or monthly income should be.

I have a very active eighty-something-year-old friend who was recently involved in a collision with another vehicle. My friend didn't want this report to appear on his auto insurance, and because the damage was estimated to cost only $500, he reasoned that with profits from an antique sale in which he was actively involved and his skills as a self-employed painter, he would have no problem paying the estimated cost. Most people who are employed on a job may find $500 an immediate hardship. But my friend, even at his age, didn't see this amount as a great sum because of his ability to determine his earning potential as an entrepreneur.

I have had the ability to travel extensively internationally and to own my home and other properties (no mortgages) because of my ability to not allow my time and earning potential to be determined by someone other than myself. Our children will emulate our example as entrepreneurs. If we want them to be independent businesspeople, we must set an example.

Step 11. Be an exemplary father for your male children.

Our oldest son was a scholar athlete and in 1999 received a nomination to the Naval Academy from our Republican and senators from the state of Missouri. As I mentioned earlier, when our son was interviewed by our local newspaper, he said his role model was his father, "because of his morals." When I read his response, I realized he had seen a quality in me that he admired and wanted others to know about. I was proud of his response, and I am proud of both our sons for their service to our country as navy officers.

We can be a positive or negative influence on the lives of our male children. The negative influence can be seen in the prison inmate mentioned earlier who asked me to wish his son, incarcerated on another floor in the same prison, a happy birthday. Our sons see their first role models in their fathers or other influential male figures in their lives.

Step 12. G-d has created the human being with excellent potential.

The realization of this potential is achievable with G-d's guidance. Seek G-d's guidance in all you do and it will appear. We should be exemplary in our own lives as people who are guided by divine principles if we want our sons to have a role model. We should tell our sons through words as well as deeds that the guidance of G-d is the only real guidance.

Step 13. With G-d's guidance and the goodwill of others, our young men can become what is inherent in their nature to become.

Our nature is inclined toward that which is good. We should emphasize to our sons that the greatest pleasure is not the pleasure of self or the pleasure of others, but the greatest of all pleasures is "the pleasure of G-d."

Chapter 5

Insanity and the Depth of Racism

These thirteen steps can certainly help us combat the effects of racism, but fundamental changes in our racist society and attitudes will require significant spiritual change in individuals and a conscious effort from all people to eradicate racial tensions and teachings.

In the latter part of 1970s, my wife and I were the owners of a small community restaurant. We were open seven days a week and served breakfast, lunch, and dinner. Our menu consisted mostly of foods that would be considered home-style cooking. Our seating capacity was not that large; we could seat approximately twenty to twenty-five people. We had a balanced sit-down and carry-out business.

Some of our customers brought their wives or children for lunch. On occasion, they noticed a young white male in our restaurant who would give them the "evil-eye stare." I knew who they were talking about, and I had spoken to Jerry, who was a resident of the insane asylum out on a day pass, not to give our customers that stare because it made them feel uneasy.

Our patience was up with Jerry when he did the same thing again and I asked him to stop. He wanted to argue with me about what he was doing. Realizing that Jerry was becoming disruptive, I asked him to leave, and I followed him out the door. When Jerry and I closed the front door, I asked him to go back to his residence (the insane asylum).

Jerry walked about twenty or thirty yards ahead of me, picked up a rock, and threw it at me, shouting, "I am better than you because I am white."

Insanity does not cure racism. Here is a man who was certifiably insane, but his insanity still saw his white skin as superior to my black skin. This man's racism was engrained in his psyche, and his mental illness didn't supersede his racial superiority complex, which is also a mental illness. (Racial superiority or inferiority is a mental illness that can be cured by thinking differently and making your thoughts and deeds one.) Racial superiority or inferiority has to be taught; it is not an inherited trait. It is a lie that is taught in religion, history, social science, and other fields and institutions of learning. We can begin to eradicate this lie by first starting with ourselves and our families with the realization that humanity is one: there is no superior or inferior race in the eyes of G-d. The best among us in his sight are those who are most conscious of G-d.

What is the color of G-d the Father? If the color of the Son is white, what are the effects on the rest of the males who are not of that color? Twenty-five years ago I traveled with the US State Department on an agricultural and business international promotional tour to countries in the Middle East and in Africa.

Our goal was to promote the growing and buying of soybean products from Midwestern farmers. There were approximately twenty to twenty-five businessmen and farmers, mostly from states in the Midwest. With the exception of myself and one naturalized citizen from the Middle East, everyone else was a white male. Before our departure, the State Department invited all to meet in Omaha, Nebraska, for a briefing on proper protocol and etiquette around people of different religions and ethics when traveling in their countries. We were warned not to be loud or obnoxious in our behavior toward anyone in those countries. We should not offend anyone or cause a problem that would cause us to be arrested or detained by authorities in any of those countries. We were told that the tour would proceed without us, and it would be up to the individual to get in touch with someone in our embassy in that country, if we were detained.

Upon hearing this talk, I knew who these remarks were aimed at, and they weren't aimed at me. Because of racial imagery, white men in America have an attitude of "privileged white male" and think that that attitude can be expressed or accepted anywhere in the world. What we were being told was that your (white) color may not be as privileged in some countries as it is in America, and that you should be conscious of that fact. We all got the message, and we were able to have a very successful and rewarding international business tour.

Perhaps it is best said in the following quotes from the Quran, 30:22 (translation by Yusef Ali): "And among his Signs is the creation of the heavens and the earth and the variations in your languages and in your colors: verily in that are signs for those who know."

From 18:88–96: "They say '(G-d) Most Gracious has gotten a son.' Indeed you have put forth a thing most monstrous.

"At it the skies are ready to burst, the earth to split asunder, and the mountains to fall down in utter ruin.

"That they should invoke a son for (G-d) Most Gracious.

"For it is not consonant with the majesty of (G-d) that he should get a son.

"Not one of the beings in the Heavens and the Earth but must come to (G-d) most gracious as a servant.

"He does take an account of the (all) and have numbered them (all) exactly.

"And every one of them will come to him singly on the Day of Judgment.

"On those who believe and work deeds of righteousness, Will (G-d) most gracious show love?"

In 39:4: "Had G-d wished to take to himself a son, He could choose whom he pleased out of those whom he did create. But glory be to him (He is above such things.) He is G-d The One, The Irresistible."

In 5:116–120:

"And behold G-d will say 'O Jesus the son of Mary, did you say unto men Worship me and my mother as gods in derogation of G-d?' He will say: 'Glory to thee, Never would I say what I had no right to say. Had I said such a thing, you would have indeed known it. You know what is in my heart, though I know not what is yours. For you know in full all that is hidden.

'Never said I to them other than what you did command me to say which was to "Worship G-d, my Lord and your Lord" and I was a witness over them while I dwelt among them ; when you did take me up you was the watcher over them and you are a witness to all things.

"If you punish them they are your servants; If you do forgive them you are the Exalted in power The Wise.

"G-d will say: 'This is a day on which the truthful will profit from their truth: theirs are gardens with rivers flowing beneath, their eternal home: G-d well pleased with them and they with G-d: that is the great Salvation. (The fulfillment of all desires).

"To G-d does belong the dominion of the heavens and the earth, and all that is therein, and it is He who has power over all things."

In 112:1–4, the Ikhlas, or Purity (of Faith)
With the Name of G-d Most Gracious, Most Merciful

1. Say he is G-d The One and Only
2. G-d, the eternal, the Absolute
3. He begets not, nor is he begotten
4. And there is none like unto him

I say these four verses to establish four of the "Best Images of G-d."

The end of the concept of racism by man: G-d says in the Quran that Prophet Muhammad is a mercy to all of humanity. His final sermon witnessed by thousands unites humanity as one and destroys any racial or ethnic superiority of one race over another.

The Prophet Muhammad's Last Sermon

This sermon was delivered on the Ninth Day of Dhu al-Hijjah 10 AH (March 9, 632) in the Uranah valley of Mount Arafat (in Mecca), during the Islamic pilgrimage of Hajj.

After praising and thanking Allah, he said:

"O People, lend me an attentive ear, for I know not whether after this year, I shall ever be amongst you again. Therefore listen to what I am saying to you very carefully and take these words to those who could not be present here today.

"O People, just as you regard this month, this day, this city as Sacred, so regard the life and property of every Muslim as a sacred trust. Return the goods entrusted to you to their rightful owners. Hurt no one so that no one may hurt you. Remember that you will indeed meet your LORD, and that HE will indeed reckon your deeds. ALLAH has forbidden you to take usury (interest), therefore all interest obligation shall henceforth be waived. Your capital, however, is yours to keep. You will neither inflict nor suffer any inequity. Allah has judged that there shall be no interest and that all the interest due to Abbas ibn 'Abd'al Muttalib (Prophet's uncle) shall henceforth be waived.

"Beware of Satan, for the safety of your religion. He has lost all hope that he will ever be able to lead you astray in big things, so beware of following him in small things.

"O People, it is true that you have certain rights with regard to your women, but they also have rights over you. Remember that you have taken them as your wives only under Allah's trust and with His permission. If they abide by your right then to them belongs the right to be fed and clothed in kindness. Do treat your women well and be kind to them for they are your partners and committed helpers. And it is your right that they do not make friends with anyone of whom you do not approve, as well as never to be unchaste.

"O People, listen to me in earnest, worship ALLAH, say your five daily prayers (Salah), fast during the month of Ramadan, and give your wealth in Zakat. Perform Hajj if you can afford to.

"All mankind is from Adam and Eve, an Arab has no superiority over a non-Arab nor a non-Arab has any superiority over an Arab; also a white has no superiority over black nor does a black have any superiority over white except by piety and good action. Learn that every Muslim is a brother to every Muslim and that the Muslims constitute one brotherhood. Nothing shall be legitimate to a Muslim which belongs to a fellow Muslim unless it was given freely and willingly. Do not, therefore, do injustice to yourselves.

"Remember, one day you will appear before ALLAH and answer your deeds. So beware; do not stray from the path of righteousness after I am gone.

"O People, no prophet or apostle will come after me and no new faith will be born. Reason well, therefore, O People, and understand words which I convey to you. I leave behind me two things, the Quran and my example, the Sunnah, and if you follow these you will never go astray.

"All those who listen to me shall pass on my words to others and those to others again; and may the last ones understand my words better than those who listen to me directly. Be my witness, O ALLAH, that I have conveyed your message to your people."

Appendix: Another Perspective by Blase Boettcher

W hen my friend Wali Furqan told me he was going to write a second book, one which would discuss the destruction and salvation of the young black male, he told me he would call it "Damaged Goods in Black and White" and asked me if I would also write about my experience dealing with young males. Wali and I lived in the same neighborhood together for over twenty years, and I have been leader of an "inner city" Boy Scout troop in that neighborhood since 1970. I declined, citing the fact that I had mainly worked with African American youngsters and really didn't have much experience with raising white youth in the city, even though he said he was talking about all young men. I did tell him that I would help him with the book, reading it and offering advice about wording, grammar, and other writing decisions. I have done that.

I have been an educator in North St. Louis and have

worked in public or parochial schools for the past forty years, in addition to working with a Boy Scout troop. Wali and I lived across the street from each other while we were both raising children, in a neighborhood that the local paper, *The St. Louis Post-Dispatch,* called the most dangerous St. Louis neighborhood in the 1990s.

As Wali's book developed and became a reality, I realized that he and I were not that far apart in our perception of the factors that could help make a male child, white or black, become a successful adult. Recently, that belief was affirmed even more when I came across an essay I had written in 1996 when I was working on my master's degree. I wrote that essay when my son was eleven years old and facing the most difficult years of his life. I would like to present that essay now, and then reflect on it afterward.

1996 Essay on Raising My Son

When he was three, my son drove his big-wheel tricycle down the stairs from the third floor, crashing onto the second-floor landing and barely escaping a slide all the way to the basement landing. When he was four, he was leaning against the car door, minus a seatbelt, and rolled out onto a busy street as we made a sharp left turn. When he was five, while we were visiting a friend at the state prison near Jefferson City, he was captivated by the clanging entrance gates, shining razor wire, impeccably uniformed guards atop the limestone towers, and their equally shiny guns; "I want to go to prison when I grow up," he told me.

He is eleven now, and I have been fighting to keep my son alive and out of trouble ever since. It hasn't been easy. It is not that he is a bad kid—in fact, he is a pretty good kid. It is just that, like most kids, as he develops and attempts to mature, he tends to make rash judgments and poor decisions. Some of them are easily ignored, but others are potentially threatening, both to his health and his freedom.

So what? you say. You made the same kind of decisions when you grew up, and you're okay. True. But it's not the same. The parameters weren't as tight back then; there was more margin for error. When I was thirteen and "got in with the wrong crowd," our worst actions were killing the neighbor's cat and breaking into a carpenter's storage shed. A parental licking and back-and-forth interactions with the juvenile authorities were the prices I paid for those decisions. Every young boy does something like that, you say. What are you whining about? Let your kid make his mistakes and everything will turn out okay.

Maybe you are right. But ... I still say it is a different time, different temptations, different consequences. Over the last twenty-five years, I have tried to help raise numerous "sons" in the classroom and in my scout troop. I have learned that this is a time and a society that doesn't tolerate the poor decision. Ricky and Kevin both didn't make it to their sixteenth birthdays because they chose to ride bicycles with no brakes. Edwin drove his mother's car into a light pole and was electrocuted trying to lift it off the front end with his bare hands. Jimmy decided to trust his best friend who told him the gun wasn't loaded. Marcus and Ray didn't think they needed that "sissy" asthma inhaler anymore. Melvin didn't like the way the guy on the corner looked at him. Melvin yelled an obscenity, and the guy fired a .38 back. Gerald and Chris believed they could outsmart their drug suppliers; for this choice, Gerald "earned" four bullets, and Chris, eighteen.

In many ways, these are the lucky ones. They paid a quick price for their mistakes and don't have to worry about making any more. Others haven't been so "lucky." Rodney breathes through a tracheotomy and walks with a limp. He is also trying to overcome the felony conviction he pleaded to when a juvenile friend stole an expensive bicycle in his presence. Tommy is on death row while Tubby and Glen are serving life sentences. Keith has only one good eye, since the other was shot out when he was attempting to rob a liquor store. Darryl has a hard time remembering where he lives—when he has enough money to stay somewhere—because most of his brain cells have turned to jelly from all the heavy drinking he has been doing since he was twelve. Bill is constantly harassed by process servers for debts he incurred before he spent five years in prison for armed robbery. (It is awfully hard to pay off loans from inside prison walls.) Tyrone just got out of federal prison and is having difficulty finding a job to help take care of himself and the four children he had by the time he was twenty.

I could go on and on, but you get the point. These weren't hardened criminals paying the price for a lifetime of bad behavior and bad choices. Not one of those I mentioned was old enough to drink legally when he made the decision that cost him his life or his freedom. They were babies, youngsters trying to grow up, but they didn't have the luxury of making a mistake.

Okay, you say, but what does that have to do with your kid? A lot of those other kids came from poor or dysfunctional families; a lot of them didn't have a stable environment or a loving family; yours does. A lot of them didn't have the educational opportunities or push that your son has. True, but some of them did. That didn't keep them from choosing unwisely, and nothing—no matter how hard I wish it or pray for it—is going to keep my kid from choosing unwisely. As a matter of fact, some of those unwise choices are going to help him grow into adulthood—if they don't kill him or incarcerate him first.

Enough, you now say. You win. It's a terrible world and a bad time to raise a kid. But it is too late now. You can't send him back, so what are you going to do about it? Well, I thought about locking him in the basement until he is thirty-three or beating the crap out of him every time he does something stupid— actually, I've come close to doing that more than once—or sending him to his grandmother's so she can take the blame when he turns out bad. However, my own ego says I can make him into a fine young man and, dammit, I am going to do just that. No matter what he thinks or what he says, I am going to make him grow up and do what is right.

Oops! There's the rub, as the old saying goes. I seem to be forgetting two basic tenets of parenthood: one, it is his life, not mine; and, two, the more you try to force a child, the more he or she fights back. (My fifteen-year-old daughter reminds me of the latter constantly.)

So, what is left to do? Surrender or accept the challenge? Sit around worrying about the double threats of death and jail, or dream and prepare for success and grandchildren (even though he has said he wants to be a priest)? The choices, my choices, are obvious. Now I have to do those things necessary so that he too can make the right choices.

First, I have to love him, no matter what. My experience with those many young men mentioned earlier has shown me that love by itself will not guarantee success, but it sure helps the healing process in times of failure. Second, I have to demand the most out of him, within reason, and not accept any less. At the same time, I must remember that it is his life to live and his choices to make, not mine. That is why, thirdly, I must do everything I can to help him learn how to make his own good decisions. When I look at those young men whose failures I chronicled, I notice that many of them were not following their own wisdom when they fell; they were listening to others.

If my son can learn to avoid the devil's tongue, then he has a chance. I remember a time when he was in first grade and threw a piece of rolled-up paper at a young lady on the other side of the room. My wife asked him why, and he replied, referring to a classmate, "Ernest made me do it." We have been working ever since to eliminate Ernest. We question, challenge, discuss, harangue, beg, and educate. Sometimes we succeed, sometimes we fail. Much is left to still accomplish in that direction.

Finally, I must learn to enjoy raising this son, despite the dangers and pitfalls. He brings me great pleasure—sometimes even when he is a pain in the butt—and often great entertainment. If I start to see him only as a potential danger and start to worry too much, then the joy and the fun will go out of our relationship, and any chance I might have to influence his decision making will disappear also.

This is not a good era in which to be growing up. Our children face many more challenges than we did at their age: many more temptations, many more negative choices, incredible technological advances, and extreme peer pressure from school and street and media. We have to do all we can to help them grow during this time and become strong young men who can stand on their own two feet and face the world that is trying to destroy them.

Reflections Eighteen Years Later

As I look back at that essay, it seems that the world of today's youth has become even more threatening: 9/11, Iraq, Afghanistan, pornographic and violent music, and Internet sites and videogames, instant messaging, social media, the Trayvon Martin and Michael Brown incidents, Syrian terrorists. The list goes on. As Wali puts it so well in his book, the forces seem to be lined up to destroy our children.

The other thing I can now see is that our efforts with our son—like Wali's with his two—have paid dividends. Our boy is now a twenty-nine-year-old educated man, working in the athletic department at Vanderbilt University in Nashville and making plans to be married. Were Wali and I just lucky? I think not. First of all, we both had strong spouses, beautiful and wonderful women, who worked with us as we raised our children. We followed the same general principles Wali mentions in his book. We emphasized humanity first. We gave our sons moral, spiritual, and socially conscious images to imitate. We encouraged reading (though our son fought reading almost all the time; it is ironic that he is now a professional journalist). We taught respect for women, even their sisters—a sometimes difficult task. We stressed using the mind at the same time we encouraged physical training and competition. Education always came first in both our houses. We never let criminal activities or gambling or drug and alcoholic usage become an option, for our sons or for us. We tried to be good role models and sought the guidance of the Divine when the real world threatened to derail us. We looked for help from our friends and neighbors and church families.

I know that sounds somewhat pretentious, self-promoting, and arrogant, and I am sorry it seems that way. The fact is that raising my children is the hardest thing I have ever done. I am lucky that my children have turned out to be good human beings. Their present condition is not because of the efforts we made—it is because of the choices they made. Our efforts only gave them a platform from which to see the consequences of their choices more clearly and have the wisdom to make the right ones. (I also know that challenges will continue to face my children as they grow older and they will have to continue to make good choices. The struggle is not over.)

I further realize, as I look back at that old essay and the youth whose failures I mentioned, that poor choices do not have to rule our lives forever. Rodney went to college, had his felony record expunged, and is working in education. He is the proud, strong, effective father of two fine young men. Glenn was paroled after twenty-three years and is leading a balanced life as a father, husband, and employee. Bill has stayed out of prison, and although still haunted by some debts, has found a career in the hospitality industry. Tyrone has started his own towing company and owns two trucks. Bad choices can be followed by good ones. As Wali says, learning should never stop.

Still, our young men today face more and more obstacles to living good, productive lives. Trayvon Martin and Michael

Brown are only tips of the iceberg. Too many of our males are being destroyed by their peers. Three weeks after the Michael Brown shooting, one of my former scouts was gunned down in the back in an alley because of an argument over a young lady. He was one of nine killed in North St. Louis in eight days, all by other young men.

So, where do we go from here? We try to follow the precepts set forth by Wali Furqan. We look out for our young men. We get involved in their lives, whether they are our sons or not. In his book Wali mentions challenging drug dealers and other negative influences in his neighborhood. We must all somehow be willing to do the same, as difficult and as dangerous as that can be. We must let our youth know that we do care how they turn out, that we don't want them dead or in prison.

Once, when my son was about eight years old, he was playing in the street around the corner from our house, acting silly and putting himself in danger. A neighbor lady yelled at him, telling him to get his "scrawny little ass out of the street." He was furious at her and came to his mother and me, telling us the story, hoping we would go tell the lady to mind her own business. Instead, we took him to Mrs. Wilson and thanked her for worrying about him and keeping him from harming himself. We encouraged her to yell at him anytime he was doing wrong or dangerous activities. As Wali makes so clear in his book, we are all brothers and sisters in the Divine plan, and we must look after each other, no matter how hard or treacherous that task becomes. We must pay attention to our youth, black or white, city or country, rich or poor. We must accept the challenge that Wali Furqan has put forth so eloquently.

Acknowledgments

I would like to thank my good friend and neighbor (for more than thirty years) Blase Boettcher for his patience and assistance in editing this book and my first book, *A Free Mind in the City.*

Thank you for your reading of this book, and may G-d reward us all according to the best of our intentions.

Endnotes

1 Miller, W. B. *Crime by Youth Gangs and Groups in the United States*, Washington, DC: US Department of Justice, Office of Justice Programs, Office of Juvenile Justice and Delinquency Prevention, 1992 (Revised from 1982).

2 Moore, J. P. and C. P. Terrett. *Highlights of the 1996 National Youth Gang Survey*, Fact Sheet, Washington, DC: US Department of Justice, Office of Justice Programs, Office of Juvenile Justice and Delinquency Prevention, 1996.

3 Bjerregaard B. and A. J. Lizotte. "Gun ownership and gang membership," *Journal of Criminal Law and Criminology* 86:3758, 1995.

4 Morales, A. "A clinical model for the prevention of gang violence and homicide," in *Substance Abuse and Gang Violence*, edited by R. C. Cervantes, Newbury Park, CA: Sage Publications, Inc., 1992, 105–118.

5 Decker, S. H. and B. van Winkle. *Life in the Gang: Family, Friends, and Violence*, New York, NY: Cambridge University Press, 1996.

6 Howell, J. C. and S. H. Decker. *The Gangs, Drugs, and Violence Connection*, Bulletin, Washington, DC: US Department of Justice, Office of Justice Programs, Office of Juvenile Justice and Delinquency Prevention, 1996.

Printed in the United States
By Bookmasters